Life

Scott Wells

BookLeaf Publishing

India | USA | UK

Presentation by *BookLeaf Publishing*

Web: www.bookleafpub.com

E-mail: info@bookleafpub.com

ISBN: 9789360941970

First edition 2024

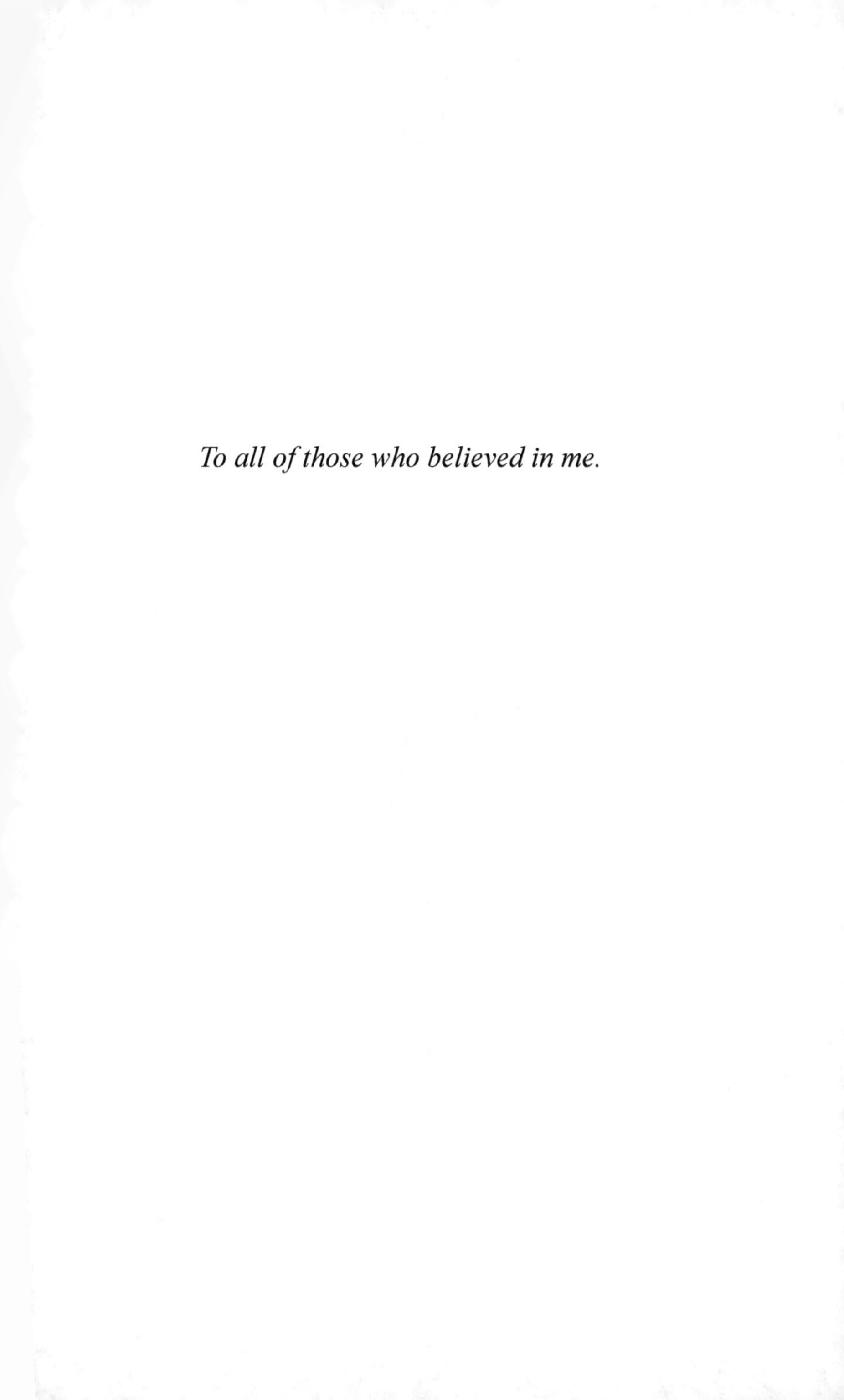

To all of those who believed in me.

The Beginning

The journey begins
From darkness to light
Labored breath and screams
Fill the room tonight

Heart stops every push
The noose is tightened
Constricting the air
Panic is heightened

A slicing of flesh
Cold hands reach inside
No death here tonight
Escape through red tide

Grasped by the ankle
And struck on the rear
Loud crying is heard
A new life is here

Age of Innocence

Voyage home complete
Time at steady pace
Everyone now gather round
Admiring smiling face

Upright on two legs
Suckling breasts has ceased
A watchful eye must be kept
Thirst for knowledge increased

Days are filled with play
Happiness and toys
These precious years limited
A thief comes for all joys

Enjoy these pleasures
Each and every day
Live in blissful ignorance
A monster comes your way

The Monster

I see a monster
When i look in the glass

With hair all over
And bumps on his face
He whispers in my ear
That they all laugh at me

Despite what they say
I believe him
Falling for his tricks every day

For in my reflection
I see his truth
I'm not what the world wants

So say what you will
Tell me it's a lie
This monster is with me
And he'll never die

Brothers

To my brothers
For my brothers
Though you do not share my blood
You have done a better job
Than any blood brother could

Through the good times
And the distance
Even through today
I'm pleased to have you in my life
Every single day

Isolation

Existing here as
a shadow
Olive drab walls close in
a fruitless passing of
grains of sand

The day, a mirror of
yesterday, a foretelling of
tomorrow
Sentenced to unknown years

The Fall

Standing with old birds
Up in the tree
The time has come
For me to be free

I watch the elders
As they take flight
I've seen them all do it
But it doesn't seem right

I put my head down
And do as they say
Just spread your wings
We've shown you the way

As I gear up
To take that big leap
I slow down my breathing
My fear pushed down deep

After my jump
Something goes wrong
I am not flying
The fall down is long

I get back up there
I'm going to win
I do what I'm told
But I'm falling again

The Future is Yours

A sacrifice of years
Preparing for life
to be sent out naked
With a paper and a handshake
Abandoned in the desert
of an unknown land
An explorer without a compass
Looking now upon the sands of time

Faithless

You've always been there
or so I'm told
And I believed it
Facts
that no child could ignore
Then clouds rolled in
Blocking the sunshine
A storm
Desperately seeking an open hand
To pull me from the flood
But nothing
I pulled myself up
Seeing upturned crosses
I walked to them
Traveling through the darkness
Alone

Bliss

The first warm night
The lilacs in bloom
The moon is my light
Suppressing my gloom

I breathe with ease
Such pleasure is rare
The cool, sweet breeze
Caressing my hair

Out in this world
My soul starts to heal
This feeling too good
It doesn't seem real

Before my wounds fully mend
My outing now abruptly ends

Chased by Death

A new feeling
out of the blue
Mortal, fragile
Sudden loss of life
a deception from within
taken as fact every time

Awakened from a dead sleep,
gasping
Taking their pills heightens my dread
all alone
At war with an invisible enemy
Every day is the last

The Flower Withers

There lives a flower
On a sill
and through neglect
she lives there still

Waiting for me
To return
and care for her
Leaves all burned

Now I'm back
Though not for long
She thinks I'm home
but she is wrong

Then one day I
Came back for good
To care for her
the way I should

Wasting Away

Unable to move, frozen
Seeing dreams just out of reach
Locked in place like concrete
Withheld from me by myself
A door barred from the other side
Set at idle, waiting
The door won't open

Unpacking Old Baggage

Buried deep in
the closet of my past
A dusty old bag
No knowledge of what's inside
Hidden, easy to ignore
A time capsule of regret
Unzipped, opened wide
The contents soiled
Now out of my mind

The Tub

Yellow liquid, bubbles dance
tub filled to the brim
A vessel to drown my
Sorrow

Turned away, work complete
leaving the dark for dead

Only it thrives, returning
with vigor
a lotus flower in
the water

Sunday Morning Drunks

Sunday morning drunks
Joking and laughing
before the world wakes up

Sunday morning drunks
Drinking and stumbling
The first thing they have done

I cook them eggs and sausage
And watch them fool around
Just one more Bloody Mary
They'll be on the ground

Sunday morning drunks
Chocking and puking
They won't give up

Sunday morning drunks
Sad and uncouth
I won't be like them

They open my eyes
To the fool that I've been
My change starts today
I'll never be like them

Hope Misplaced

Summon me
Take away this pain
Onward marching in misery
No end in sight

Summon me
You can unlock the door
What awaits past threshold see
Hopeful that it's bright

Summon me
Your promises are lies
The glorious future that be
Devoid of light

Kill me
Expectations high
Your employ is an endless sea
Meant to swallow my dreams

Kill me
Some things never change
Predictions have not come to be
Fooled again it seems

Kill me
This cycle will not cease
With cruelty you ignore my pleas
Hear my soul, it screams

The Mountain

Oh, here on the mountain
What a terrible place
Why was I brought here
Why have I stayed
The dregs march the streets
Throughout day and night
Picking up cans
For their really nice treat

Here on the mountain
My seat on the porch
Watching the sadness
Flowing in the gutter
Worse every day
No hope in sight
Be sure to wave
I beg you, don't stay

The Transporter

Upon entering the institution
In the dead of night
I confer with a stranger
'Neath artificial light

With everything in order
You belong to me
I'm led to your room
Wherein many now sleep

The smell here is horrid
You've been here awhile
All are on racks
Organized like files

You're brought down to me
I know who you are
And though I now move you
We're not going far

Gripping your dressing
Now I gently tug
You're on a new bed
Belted in snug

Back in the van
we don't skip a beat
Here is your last home
My work is complete

I won't say a word

It's dark, it's cold, it's quiet
I won't say a word
I've been cut wide open
I won't say a word
Thick threads cross my chest
I won't say a word
A zipper took the light away
I won't say a word
Despite being moved around
I won't say a word
Even after two long rides
I won't say a word
What is that noise
I won't say a word
Engulfed in flames
I won't say a word

Ungovernable

It's said the grass is greener
Yet a short walk through town
Reveals every lawn peppered with excrement
And fools who walk blindfolded, smiling
With nothing covering their feet
Upon asking why
They beckon me to join them
Facing exile from their society
Recalling all that I have seen
I gladly turn my back to them
Leaving those poor souls behind
I forge a new path unlike theirs
For I too have set foot on those lawns
But I've removed my blindfold

Break the Chains

Lift your head
Stand up, feel your potential
Break the chains
Tethering you to a meaningless life

Riding the coattails
Of those in power, hoping they have the key
Is the philosophy of fools
For they have thrown the key away
Hoping to keep you bound, generating their
selfish wealth
For the money doesn't flow downhill
It's carried to the top, by those with calloused
hands
Only to be kicked back to the bottom
For the cycle to begin anew

To end the cycle
You must look fear in the eyes
For ruin is a construct of man
To steal your dreams and keep you in line